# Miscegenation Round Dance
## poèmes historiques

### Rain Prud'homme

Introduction by: Jeffery Darensbourg

2021

FIRST EDITION, 2021

Miscegenation Round Dance: póems historiques
© 2021 by Rain Prud'homme-Cranford

ISBN 978-1-7323935-8-5

Except for fair use in reviews and/or scholarly considerations, no part of this book may be reproduced, performed, recorded, or otherwise transmitted without the written consent of the author and the permission of the publisher.

Cover Art: "Mom hoktiwe pumblo! (Let's all dance together!)"
© 2020 by Rain Prud'homme-Cranford and EL Kiki Shawnee

Author Photo
@2019 by T. Shawnee

Family photographs: @2020 courtesy of the author's parents

Mongrel Empire Press
Norman, OK

Online catalogue: www.mongrelempire.org

Dedication:

For Home, Soil, & Family.

Mési/ Hiweyú/ Yakoke/ Tikahch/ Maarsii/ Tapadh leibh/ Mvto/ Thank you

With thanks to my family (in blood and made) and friends who have supported and read various incarnations of this collection.

*In Memoriam of Granddaddy and Mama Janet*

# Track List

Dedication
Acknowledgements
**Introduction:** "More than Shake Hands"..........................i
**Prologue:** Hatwan: Orison..........................2

## I. Miscegenation Blues

Historical Codes and Observations: A Found Poem..........................4
Loom..........................6
Red River Moan..........................7
Cane River Tanka I..........................8
Bayuk..........................9
Jeanne and Marie Anne Therese de la Grand Terre to Marie Thérèse CoinCoin..........................10
Speaking Bondage..........................11
Bundles..........................15
Misbegotten..........................16
Cane River Tanka II..........................22
Prayer for Sinners..........................23
How Turtle Begins to Relearn her Language..........................24
Apocryphal blues..........................25

## II. Uncle Jim Two-Steps

Historical Codes and Observations II: A Found Poem..........................28
Poème pour Tonton Jim..........................30
Cathoindian..........................32
Levee Womb Blues..........................33
Chitlins no More..........................34
Opelousas, September 28 1868..........................35
Love Song for Paracolonial Occupation..........................37
Footnotes on Decoding Louisiana Racial Subtexts..........................38
Poem for Mary Edmonia Lewis (1844-1907)..........................39
Dr. Frankenstein and the BIA..........................40
Love Poem for Jim Crow..........................42

Mixedblood Girls I..........................................................................43
Going Home.................................................................................44

## III. A'Capella Rattle Songs

Removals and Relocations.........................................................47
Cartography: Self Help...............................................................48
Dust Bowl Blues..........................................................................49
Tiny Tots......................................................................................50
Tongue.........................................................................................51
Mixedblood Girls II....................................................................52
Testimony: A Song......................................................................53
Fish Guts......................................................................................55
Oklahoma Ghazel.......................................................................56
Down by the River.....................................................................57
Hugs and kisses/Besos y abrazos.............................................58
Shaking Lodge............................................................................59
Rising Sun...................................................................................60

## IV. Zydeco Stomp Dances

Removals and Relocations II....................................................63
Issish/San....................................................................................65
Muscle Shoals Kinda Love.......................................................67
How to Write A NDN Country-Western Zydeco 2-Step......69
Taste / Speak...............................................................................71
Electric Muscadine....................................................................73
Rituals of Morning Water.........................................................74
What I Know..............................................................................75
If'n I Wuz Your Pocahontas Marie Laveau............................77
Keeping Away Bundle...............................................................79
Miscegenation Round Dance..................................................80
Sweeping Away..........................................................................83
Palms Open-Face.......................................................................84

**Biographies**...........................................................................85
**Notes**......................................................................................87

## Acknowledgments

With thanks to the editors of the following journals and anthologies in which these poems, sometimes in different forms, have appeared:

"Bayuk" *Sugar Mule: Women Writing Nature* Issue
"Cane River Tanka I" and "Cane River Tanka II" as: "Cane River Tankas" *Future
        Earth Magazine: Reflections on Natasha Tretheway*
"Cathoindian" *The Mas Tequila Review #10*
"Dust Bowl Blues" *As Us: A Space for Women of the World*
"Fish Guts" *Yellow Medicine Review*
"Loom" *As Us: A Space for Women of the World*
"Love Poem for Jim Crow." *Future Earth Magazine: Reflections on
        Natasha Tretheway*
"Love Song for Paracolonial Occupation" *The Mas Tequila Review
        #10*
"Misbegotten" *Tidal Basin Review*
"Miscegenation Round Dance" *Tidal Basin Review: Cultural Pride
        Issue*
"Oklahoma Ghazel" *Plume*
"How Turtle Begins to Relearn her Language" *Plume*
"Palms Open-Face" *Bulbancha Is Still a Place: Indigenous Culture
        from New Orleans*
"Poème pour Tonton Jim" *Tidal Basin Review*
"Red River Moan" *Rabbit and Rose Journal*, Issue V
"Rituals of Morning Water" *The Lake Rises*
"Sweeping Away" *Rabbit and Rose Journal*, Issue VII
"What I Know" *Tidal Basin Review: Cultural Pride* Issue
"Taste/Speak" *Sovereign Traces II: Relational Constellation*
"Electric Muscadine" *Sovereign Traces II: Relational Constellation*
"Mixedblood Girls II" *Anomaly*

# Introduction
## "More than Shake Hands"
### Jeffery Darensbourg

In the titular poem of this collection, "Miscegenation Round Dance," Rain Prud'homme offers a bold assertion of an identity that is blended, interwoven, "braided." It is also singular, taking place as one of many cultural legacies of colonialism worldwide, but happening in one particular place, Louisiana and the surrounding Gulf Coast:

> Woven brackish blood, braided carries memory for all my relations.
> Weavings like basketry, strand for Euro, one Africa, third Indian Nations.
> Into a circle we moved to dance, taking partners, making alliances for survival.
> Delicate plans, fragile treaties' offspring, crumbled under statehood's arrival.

These are "poèmes historiques," she notes, exploring history both collective and deeply personal. All humans live with such histories, in ways often unacknowledged, but in Louisiana one is called upon to think about such things in ways unavoidable. This can happen when one hears "Louisiana French" from the mouths of those whose ancestry is more than *just* European, or when one encounters certain Carnival traditions. Louisiana is one of the United States of America, but as one moseys south in *the state*, one can encounter cultures born of interactions centuries before 1776. These interactions have resulted in peoples and histories that have too often been ignored or misconstrued. In the case of Indigenous Peoples, these histories have been either erased or explained only by outsiders, often overlooking Indigenous People who are often called by regional terms that sometimes obscure their Indigeneity, in this way mimicking terms such as "Latinx" or "Puerto Rican."

From the earliest colonial encounters in the region, one can make out individual strands of the braids of mixed ethnicity emerging. In 1699 Pierre le Moyne, sieur d'Iberville, led a group of Frenchmen up the Mississippi River to a place known as Bulbancha, "the place of other tongues," a linguistically dense area of cultural interaction between Indigenous Nations at a congruence of waterways that the French would later attempt to rename "New Orleans."[1] (I say "attempt" because there are still people in the city where I live, myself included, who stalwartly use the original name.) Upon arrival, they noticed bison napping on the shore, a road from the river to nearby Bayou Choupique- I use this term instead of the vulgar "Bayou St. John;"- and found members of the Biloxi Nation doing a controlled burn of a prairie. River cane, *uski /oski*, used to make blowguns, flutes, and countless other items, abounded. Before departing the area, Iberville planted some seeds of sugarcane in what would become the French Quarter neighborhood, seeds he had brought with him from the French colony of Saint-Domingue.[2] The French had already brought enslaved Africans to that Caribbean colony. They would gain freedom in a glorious revolution a century later. Even though these Africans were not present on that day in 1699, the plans were already in place to import human beings for the rough work of growing and processing sugar for the profit of others. The French assumed they owned the place. These interactions between Indigenous, Europeans, and Africans form the situational basis of Louisiana Creole identity- a post contact Afro-Indigenous people.

---

[1] The various spellings of the word coincide with differing orthographies of a mostly oral language. Here I use *Bulbancha* as this was the first spelling I learned, taken from the first published Choctaw dictionary, Chief Allen Wright's *A Chahta Leksikon: Choctaw in English Definition for the Choctaw Academies and Schools* (St. Louis: Presbyterian Publishing, 1880). For comments on the spelling see Hali Dardar, "Bvlbancha," 64 *Parishes*, Fall 2019, 22.

[2] Cf. Richard Campanella, *Bienville's Dilemma: A Historical Geography of New Orleans* (Lafayette: University of Louisiana Press, 2008) pp. 105-108.

As these peoples combined over and over again, the Indigenous aspects of Creole culture were often ignored. On November 5th, 1961, a bronze statue was dedicated at the site of St. Martin de Tours Catholic Church in St. Martinville, Louisiana, a statue commemorating the original inhabitants of the area, the Ishak, more commonly known by a word given from outside the tribe, "Atakapa" (in various spellings).[3] The statue is located in a town that was a centerpiece of the Attakapas District under French and Spanish rule. This statue, which still stands, is based on one of the earliest colonial images of Natives in Louisiana, a 1735 watercolour by French polymath Alexandre DeBatz. The inscription on its plinth reflects a typical sentiment about the Ishak, my people: "a roving savage tribe who settled here prior to the French, partly Christianized and civilized by missionaries."[4]

This banner event of the statue's unveiling featured many local white-identified inhabitants~Wink, wink~ wearing "at least an Indian headband with a cocky feather." It also included "Indians who still live in the area," namely, people from the federally recognized Chitimacha Nation, as well as members of the Coushatta Nation, a decade before their own reestablishment of federal recognition. The keynote address was given by deLesseps Morrison, at the time U.S. Ambassador to the Organization of American States. Notably absent in Morrison's remarks, which centered on the purported triumph of the interests of the Kennedy Administration in Latin America, or in any published account of the ceremony, were the Ishak ourselves.[5]

---

[3] "Thousands Brave Inclement Weather to Join in Indian Day Celebration in St. Martinville Last Sunday," *Teche News* (9 November 1961) p. 1.
[4] Regarding the DeBatz image, see Katie A. Pfohl, "In Land, Sea: Louisiana's Shifting Landscape," in Katie A. Pfohl, ed., *Inventing Acadia: Painting and Place in Louisiana* (New Haven: Yale University Press, 2019) pp. 23-25. For my own, personal take on this image, see Jeffery U. Darensbourg, "Traveling Light," *Situate* (June 2016), situatemagazine.com/issue/new-orleans/409/traveling-light.
[5] deLesseps Morrison, "Attakapa Indians Monument Dedication - St. Martinsville, Louisiana, 1961 November 5," [sic.] Special Collections

Apparently, we had ceased to exist, allegedly disappearing some decades previous. To some authors, we do not exist if we are mixed with African ancestry. In 1959, one such author identified a few "degenerate descendants" reported to be living in Franklin, Louisiana.[6] Later publications would simply skirt the question of living Ishak altogether.[7] We live this in ourselves, this notion that who we are, who we know we are, doesn't exist to many who write about us. We are forced to be phantoms in the world of the living. Yet in the very same St. Martinville were Ishak inhabitants in 1961, as there are to this day. They are sometimes called "Creole," "Black," or remain "mixed" by others.

Were I organizing the event, I might have invited a zydeco musician from Carencro, less than an hour's drive away, one Fernest Arceneaux, himself both Louisiana Creole and Ishak.[8] During that segregated time, it wouldn't have occurred to white officialdom to invite him or other Ishak. The Ishak of old called themselves that because their ancestors did, and so do the Ishak of today. That has not changed, even if we have African and European ancestors as well. We exist; we are aware of who we are.

In fact, Louisiana has a long history of classifying Natives as "Free People of Colour" or "mulatto," or even "white" instead of "Indian" or related terms, when convenient to the state.[9] Andrew

---

Division, Tulane University / deLesseps S. Morrison papers / Organization of American States, 1961-1963 / Box 211, Folder 3. Morrison was likely tapped for this task as sometime mayor of occupied Bulbancha.

[6] Harry Lewis Griffin, *The Attakapas Country: A History of Lafayette, Louisiana* (Gretna, La.: Pelican, 1959) p. 9.

[7] E.g., Joseph T. Butler, Jr. "Atakapa Indians: Cannibals of Southwest Louisiana," *Louisiana History* 11(2) (1970) pp. 167-176.

[8] Bruce Sunpie Barnes, et al., *Le Kèr Creole: Creole Compositions & Stories from Louisiana* (Bulbancha: L'Union Creole and the Neighborhood Story Project, 2019) p. 70

[9] An important recent work on this issue, especially as it relates to chattel slavery, is Leila K. Blackbird, *Entwined Threads of Red and Black: The*

Jolivétte, himself a Louisiana Creole and member of the Atakapa-Ishak Nation, argues that tribes that are heavily creolized "still exist, only now they exist as complex populations with important historical, political, social, and cultural relevancy to understanding mixed-race Native Americans in contemporary U.S. society."[10]

There is therefore a deeply healing quality about this book Dr. Prud'homme has written. It tells the stories that people have lived, stories of people negotiating their own bloodlines and culture outside of categories both easy and false. It tells of deep loss, generational suffering, but also of cultural resurrection. In my conversations with the Acadian writer David Cheramie, of Lafayette, Louisiana, he has sometimes used a phrase about interactions between those who ended up in this part of the Gulf South: "They did more than shake hands." The poetry herein captures those more intimate interactions and their legacies in a unique way. Consider these lines from "Red River Moan":

> Red skin, red blood, bodies break, bodies take, mewl calls
> Chitimacha, Natchez, Lipan, Wichita to slave,
> us Cadeaux, Choctaw, Ishak sex make.

Dr. Prud'homme tells of this because it is what happened. It is not something to whisper. It is what was, and through the descendants of these encounters, what is.

In the poem "Footnotes on Decoding Louisiana Indigenous & Racial Subtexts" one finds anecdotal exegesis of ethnic terms in

---

*Hidden History of Indigenous Enslavement in Louisiana, 1699-1824*, M.A. Thesis, University of New Orleans, 2018. A detailed critical examination of ethnic categories and effects on the tribal recognition process in Louisiana may be found in Brian Klopotek, *Recognition Odysseys: Indigeneity, Race, and Federal Tribal Recognition Policy in Three Louisiana Indian Communities* (Durham, N.C.: Duke University Press, 2011).

[10] Andrew J. Jolivétte, *Louisiana Creoles: Cultural Recovery and Mixed-Race Native American Identity* (Lanham: Lexington Books, 2007) p. 2.

Louisiana. It's a piece that gives me the *frissons*, as we say in Crenglish: a tingling excitement. It gives me this as someone who is often, though not always, white-passing, but whose 1972 Louisiana birth certificate lists both of my parents as "negro." When I would speak Louisiana French in New Roads, Louisiana, with my late maternal grandfather, Joseph Clifton Fabre, Sr., I noticed the ethnic categories he used. There were *Cadiens* (Acadians/Cajuns), *sauvages* (Natives, including some of his immediate ancestors who helped to raise him), *nègres* (usually African Americans who didn't speak French or lacked the appearance of mixed ancestry), *Américains* (miscellaneous non-Francophone white people), and finally, what we were, *nous-autres*. In Louisiana French it means simply "we," "us," whoever we might happen to be.[11] He seldom used the word "Creole," even when referring to one of his twin first languages, also known as *Kouri-Vini*, and then usually only when referring to ourselves with people outside of our community.

There was something truly *Native* about the designation "nous-autres." In Ishakkoy, for example, one of the self-designations for Ishak people is *Yukhiti*, a word that means something along the line of "the we people," or rather, "the people we are."[12] It speaks to a mystery that refuses to be confined by words, a mystery that achieves true definition only within certain human bodies. Attempts to simplify it run into music and dancing and foodways that cannot be contained. The terms we use aren't meaningless, but their meanings are scaffolded beneath waters opaque and silted. Dr. Prud'homme's definition of "white" as "my ancestors are relatively new to Louisiana" is among the most accurate I've ever seen. After several generations here, anyone's ancestors have

---

[11] Albert Valdman et al., *Dictionary of Louisiana French: As Spoken in Cajun, Creole, and American Indian Communities* (Jackson: University Press of Mississippi, 2009) s.v. "nous-autres." My thanks to David Cheramie for looking this up for me while I didn't have access to it under quarantine.

[12] David Kaufman, *Atakapa-Ishakkoy Dictionary* (Chicago: Exploration Press, 2019) s.v. "yukhiti."

done more than shake hands with the folks 'cross the bayou. This is reflected in the following collection through a history of post contact Afro-Indigeneity as Prud'homme creates something new and wholly Gulf centric... Indigenous or Creole-Indian, tracing the ways poetic form (from the bop and villanelle, to stomp songs and pantoum), language (Ishak, Choctaw, Creole, Spanish, and French), and land, communal, and personal histories come together in this space of poetic miscegenation.

In the prologue poem to the collection Prud'homme offers us a *hatwan*, the Ishak word for prayer. It is both recipe and recitation. Its construction or delivery at once echoes Ishak and Choctaw medicine making with the pestle and mortar, as well as Louisiana Voodoo, and Hoodoo. She writes:

    light three candles anointed with ashes
    from prayers burned in supplication

    add roux made from
    45 years of tears
    pound of my belly fat
    and moon time blood

        This medicine is combustible.

And so it is, a live, active, living thing within the bodies and words of our Peoples here...a fire.

It is my hope that readers who read and reread these poems will leave this textual patch of Delta dirt different than when they arrived, and that they will better appreciate their own relationship to personal and ethnic history. The first person to publish a book about Louisiana was Antoine-Simon Le Page du Pratz, whose 1758 *Histoire de la Louisiane* describes his interactions with a Chitimacha woman he kept in bondage.[13] While she seems to have been fond of him, and taught him things about the area, he

---

[13] (Paris: De Bure, 1758) pp. 82-83.

neither names her nor fully credits her work. *Miscegenation Round Dance*, however, is a volume of names, of naming specific traumas, specific peoples, and collective survivals. In the poem "Jeanne and Marie Anne Thérèse de la Grand Terre to Marie Thérèse CoinCoin," the enslavement of Chitimacha women is told from the other side, with both their names and histories. In this instance and so many others, the poems in this book lovingly pay honor to ancestors who have passed down their survival wisdom to our time. It amplifies that wisdom, which is what our mixed Creole Indigenous People truly deserve.[14]

~ Jeffery Darensbourg (Atakapa-Ishak, Alligator Clan)
Bulbancha, 2019

---

[14] A most sincere *hiwew* to the workers at A Studio in the Woods, a project of Tulane University, were I was a writer in residence during quarantine for the composition of this piece, including Cammie Hill-Prewitt, Ama Rogan, Grace Rennie, David Baker, and Joe Carmichael. I extend a *hiwew* also to Christine Baniewicz.

# Prologue

**Hatwan: Orison**

Flesh of mother
flesh of father
tongue cut from this daughter

      Tease out sorrow

juice of lemon
seeds of pomegranate
four black muscadines

      Red river water colour of rust

sea salt and turtle claw
fisher crow foot
white egret feather

      My right dead ovary

buckeye and sassafras root
witch hazel and mint
red dirt and soft clay

      Ghost memory of his seed

light three candles anointed with ashes
from prayers burned in supplication

add roux made from
46 years of tears
pound of my belly fat
and moon time blood

      This medicine is combustible

# I. Miscegenation Blues
"There's plenty more sound just like me down home"
—Mahalia Jackson

## Historical Codes and Observations: A Found Poem [i]

>We did not go to seek them
>they asked for land of us
>because their country was too little.

(They came)
permit(ing)
exercise of the Roman Catholic creed **only**.
    Forbid(ing)
(their) white subjects,
of both sexes, to marry with
    the blacks
    (and Indians),
under the penalty of
PUNISHMENT.

>We told them they might take land where they pleased;
>~~there was enough for them and for us;~~
>it was good that the same Sun should shine upon us both,
>~~that we would walk as friends in the same path;~~

Every other mode of worship
    **prohibited**
(Yoruba, Coyocop-chill)
Negroes placed
<sub>under</sub> direction
        <sub>supervision</sub> of any other
person than a Catholic... liable to confiscation.

>What occasion had we for Frenchmen?
>Before they came we live(d) better than we do,
>(they) deprive ourselves of a part of our corn,
>our game, and fish

(They came)
forbid(ing) all curates, priests,

secular or regular clergy,
(They came)
forbid(ing)
white subjects and manumitted or
free-born
Blacks
(and Indians),
to live in a state of concubinage

>	I am fine before arrival of French
>	we lived like ***HUMANS***
>	who are satisfied with we have
>		now we are like slaves

**Loom**

this solid form
       broke
              s-t-r-e-t-c-h-e-d
forth across worn loom and
       waited

fingers crooked with age of wanting
       to point
       with sureness
       for a future without
            rivets,
took to its surface

covering the dried hide in
mosaic pattern appliqué beads
whose bright colours belie
       ache in hands
       worn raw and shadowed
       displaced spirit

standing on sideline waiting to be
            **corporal**
again wrapped in loom-worked skin
solid dressings for
       strange
knowledge left hanging from
       southern tree

removed to silent schoolyard
where death taught
            f/r/a/c/t/i/o/n/s
in the lengths of hair and

       bible : verses

# Red River Moan

Gathered in voice we emerge from this river
scuffling calls like water on banks till new
mewing cries bent bodies of bare breasted
women roped, netted like baskets of crayfish.
Red clay like me, our own men come to trade
at Fort St. Jean Baptiste aux Natchitoches.

*Is that sunshine his pathway may cover*
*And the grief of the Red River Girl.*[ii]

Red skin, red blood, bodies break, bodies take, mewl calls
Chitimacha, Natchez, Lipan, Wichita to slave,
us Cadeaux, Choctaw, Ishak sex make.
Just shy ninety years click by and planters of cotton and cane,
slaves, and gens de couleur libres count us in their blood,
over half that number runs other Indian slave blood.
Black bodies cost, but Lipan woman only 50 dollars.[iii]
Red skin, red blood, bodies break, bodies take, sex breaks.
Chitimacha, Natchez, Lipan, Wichita to slave,
us Cadeaux, Choctaw, Ishak mewl calls.

*Is that sunshine his pathway may cover*
*And the grief of the Red River Girl.*

We emerged from this river, made of red
clay, broke from earth and water— struggled to
breathe, and yet our wrists still harbor rope burn.
Our cries trembling blue notes like muscadine
skin. While you have wandered into the sun, the
blood in our women warbles a red river moan.

## Cane River Tanka I
*for Tracey*

Gray water laps shore
      cattails, river cane, egrets
stand, against times ebb
         in green lands red memory
             lives like kafi and gumbo

## Bayuk

Cypress legs sunk in ageless forgotten waters.
Mammoths dressed in dusty wooly
Spanish moss dancin in sticky sultry
heat.

Meandering snake bird winds way like
water moccasin through black green algae alligator
enclave waters. Shadowed light plays against
shades of gray and chartreuse, sienna and a navy
so deep as to be licorice.

Under water, under black shilup moves
with bones collected so far back human
memory has forgotten names of ancestors fallen,
taken maimed and lost—slipped through spaces,
in-between, where stitches in the time of now,
and then, and the time to come meet.

Woven into water a basket of bone,
blood, and spirit whispers. Braided
along banks into the ridges of clay
and red earth. Breath calls up
story as winds scatter over
bayou water and muddy soils.
Soft persistent effort lest we be
forgotten.

## Jeanne and Marie Anne Thérèse de la Grand Terre to Marie Thérèse CoinCoin[iv]

Speak plain easy when eyes look back and forwards
across shared river o'cane bound in space.
We are tied to this land, our children work
return, like blood beaten slaves rising tides
ghosts in blood. They conjure us through
pricked fingers and slack rosaries.

*Prenez la donc, couleur des cendres,*
*Parce que c'est la plus triste couleur*[v]

St. Cosme fell bringing down Moses and so
Bienville's duped Gulf warriors, with St. Dennis,
and François brought thunder, fire, took us to slave.
Torn from arms at Mobile, onto Natchitoches.
Two years, splayed tattered grooves kneeling
as in prayer. Tell us Marie, is it an acquired worn
into love? Do our bodies become houses for new
races in defiance, or is it true *that we love?*

*Prenez la donc, couleur des cendres,*
*Parce que c'est la plus triste couleur*

Widening gyre our offspring's move mistakes
made like lashes on your back to mine, and yet
something prefers sienna and cardamom over talc.
I see them rise stand combined Indian-African
slave blood evening tide survivals in seventh generation.
Do you feel the earth rumble? See the cresting hurricane?

## Speaking Bondage

I.
French Colonial Archives
Natchitoches Parish
relatives generations past.
18<sup>th</sup> century faded chipped painted relation.
19<sup>th</sup> century sepia toned memory—
Her great Nanan was a bastard
granddaughter of Falamahtubby.
Tied to Cane River to Métoyer
all the way back to CoinCoin.
All our relations. Tabulated lists of
"Procurations" and "Agreements."
Desirous with wanting to know
what was silenced on black white pages.
Ancestors names passed in agreement
to agreement move— Sometimes
she reads manumission—more times sale of slave.

II.
How many ways removed from violence
Am I through the language of poetry?
Making pretty artistic euphemisms
for splayed legs, tearing labia,
ripping walls of feminine houses.
Renaming histories and transactions,
where bare breasted women
polish wood blocks in bare feet,
turning dances of bondage.

Words made a callous on my tongue.
Years of saying word rape.
One day I didn't recognize, callous
dried up fallin off —litl'bit'a
discarded memory I grown too tough
to admit was ever part of me—
Leaving stigma to other ancestors.

Easier say my grandma, my great grandma.
Violence just something imposed
on people I come from. Just inheritance.
Like MeeMa's hips or
Nanan's sturdy back.

III.
Poring over ancestors' documents,
a relative grants manumission
to slave, while purchasing others.
A brother sues a cousin, both
gens de couleur libres, for debts owed.
Red-Black blood forgotten in transactions
of bodies— of dollars— of land.

She wonders at perversions of power.
Granting freedom to bodies and enslaving them.
Suing cousins and disinheriting children.
French and Spanish rule gone. American perversion
permeating porous parishes. Did it leak into our flesh?
Is our inability to reconcile past— light-skin guilt?
Fair skin and green eyes, at odds with never
being brought up knowing life without colour—
Its violence—A need to clutch
survival from blood stained thighs.

IV.
I go to speak *this* word
far more vicious than
any other four-letter word.
Piss, Shit, Fuck, *Rape* is foulest.
Spoken in uncertain moments I'm bare
my tongue begins to bleed—
blood flowing from mouth.
Try to swallow so it don't seep
from corners of lips, like blood
flowering down broken thighs.
Trying to swallow blood back

into my body—because blood is
what it all comes down to—

V.
One drop o' blood, three-eighths-blood,
one-eighth-blood— can't afford to loose blood.
Cuz end of day, eyes of law it be blood
not culture that writes us. Not her culture
that rises up from land into people beating
into her feet rooted in red soil and Gulf air—
givin sustenance to remain—

VI.
Choctaw society rape was met with death or
with banishment. MeeMa,'s hips
broad like hers, moving family
across generations. From Sabine
to Marksville, early 20$^{th}$ century.
Before that, her apokni from Mississippi.
Her grandchildren birthed somewhere
along muddy banks of Red River—
their mother from Marksville and Natchitoches.
Her mother from Opelousas and Point Coupee.
Her father's father from Terrebonne.
Riveted blood mingled
in this story tangled and beaten, blood
strengthened by Red-Black roots. Children, putting
heads down as Jim's long shadow draws shame,
throwing away histories of violence
like a stone thrown in river.

Concentric circles spiraling ever
outward from its epicenter.
As if there is ever a justification for
rape, for beating, for rape, for beating.
That death and banishment were
still an option. Are we not still Indigenous?

VII.
She, and I, and we speak our names
in litany of names of women raped
following mother, aunt, sisters,
grandmother, great grandmothers.
Long lines of brown and red women
desecrated— Culture rooting us,
unites us. Keeps us strong so
calluses grow back—

Till they dry-up fall off and bleed.
But problem ain't the callous
problem scab under callous
and wound never healed.

# Bundles

Wrapped, tied with twine
Cocoon of soft worn
White doe hide
Egret feather
Raven feather
Eagle fluffs.
Turtle bones
Alligator tooth
Cedar
Ash
Sweetgrass
Tobacco
Stone

Unnamed pieces of appeal
Snuggled into worn white flesh...
Old photograph worn yellow
Frayed from fingers of holding
Memory too tightly.
Pray in silence of twilight

Pain is a bundle in belly
I unroll several times a week
putting in bits of memory, or reason, feeding
with salty tears and fat round words
dripping sorrow.

## Misbegotten
*A "found" poem, historic familial and re-imagined*

### I.
**misbegotten** [misbə'gätn]
adj
    1. unlawfully obtained misbegotten gains
    2. of, or relating to, or being a child or children born to unmarried parents.
    3. badly conceived, planned, or designed a misbegotten scheme.
    4. also misbegot [misbə'gätn]*Literary and dialect* illegitimate; bastard

War was ragged, had been raged, and colours had melded together, rising, rising, rising in a tidal wave of blood blending flowing in triracial colour. Fruit of misbegot schemes, and liaisons fell to finding their own survival, woven between blood, lies, lands stolen, bought and sold. War: uprising. Natchez Indians and African Slaves, between 1729-1731— Fallout ripples of repercussion throughout Mississippi delta plains, down along wandering bayuks and crescent cities. Colour changes the narrative again in Lwizyàn.

### II.
**heir** [er]
n.
    1. a person legally entitled to the property or rank of another on that person's death.
    "his eldest son and heir."
    2. a person who will legally receive money, property, or a title from another person, especially an older member of the same family, when that other person dies.

The Monsieur Valentin Sr had the audacity to die without a legal male heir. Late 18$^{th}$ century, in the heat of future Mississippi and Louisiana sun, Monsieur Valentin Sr, lay in his bed, pallid and weak, the faint smell of sweat, overly sweet sugar and acidic laudanum falls through hot wet saturation of stale air. The papers are signed. The doctor exits, and Valentin Sr's brother enters the room, joining his sister-in-law, whose piled lack luster blonde hair drips over her short pale, fine lined forehead. She clutches a frothy lace square, dabbing at the perspiration that trickles down her neck, with translucent blue veined fingers. The door shuts. Bébé is down stairs, her hair hidden under a brightly saffron tigon. Her hands rough and dark are aged beyond her thirty-six years. Her eyes gleam like obsidian in her vermillion face as she calmly lays out fresh fruits for the family, keeping eye on her son, skulking under the banana palm in the side yard. Her son, Monsieur Valentin Jr., is almost, yet shy of being his own man. His hat covers the fine curl of dark brown hair and in his olive face his eyes shimmer almost green, catching the chartreuse fire of his surroundings. He and his mother have been removed from his father's sick bed, at the request of his mother's mistress. He has no mistress. Misbegot bastard that he is, he is free. Five years later, Monsieur Valentin Jr, has come into his property. Papers signed. At twenty the land and slaves are his. His mother is moved into the big house. A year later, before the century turns, his uncle has seen the local magistrate.

## III.

**verdict:** (vûr′dĭkt)
n.
    1. Law the finding of a jury in a trial.
    2. An expressed conclusion; a judgment or opinion
    synonyms; judgment, opinion.

The brother of Valentin Sr, is awarded his nephew's land. Due to the misbegotten nature of the liaison between Valentin Sr and his half African, half Natchez slave, Bébé. In the court records it is noted that the land could not be left to a savage, not because the son was quarter black, but because his mother was half Natchez Indian.

## IV.

**mestizo** [mĕs-tē′zō]
*n. pl.* **mes·ti·zos** or **mes·ti·zoes**
    A person of mixed racial ancestry, especially of mixed European and Native American ancestry.

Who are you? Light skinned, green-eyed woman whose features at once harken the rolling hills of Ireland and the crisp hills of Scotland, bayous and palms of Gulf coast and Southern Indians, the shores of West Africa and the windy high plains of Saskatchewan and Alberta First Nations? Reciting the names, calling upon ancestors to light the thread of her life woven into a cast net, red, black and white... Thrown into the cosmos, drawing down the stars whose light greeted her ancestors as they crossed borders, racial divides, ignoring laws of miscegenation in favor of lust, of love, and even of rape–

Mestizo comes from the Latin, mixticius; meaning mixed. In lands occupied by the Spanish colonization project, the term was used to define individuals of mixed European and Indian ancestry.

**V.**
**Griffe:** 1. a person of three quarters African blood;
        2. the child of a mulatto and an African
        3. the child of a mulatto and an Indian.

Height of Indian Removal, Tennessee. Sarah's mother was listed in census document simply as a Tennessee Indian (most likely Chickasaw). Sarah went to Kentucky, and from Kentucky to Louisiana, working as a domestic. She ironed with a precession that earned her the nickname, "Straight Seam Sarah," among her employers. She was a prettish sort of girl, a little too wide of face, too stocky, too heavy of bosom and buttocks to be called truly attractive. Sarah was careful to wear a hat when hanging laundry or going to market, never letting her skin achieve more than sun kissed golden olive hue. Her eyes were wide set, dark pools that reminded men of a doe, as did her fawn coloured hair, braided and secured atop her head. She shocked the town, leaving her employer, to marry. Sarah's husband was an educated "country" doctor, and a free person of colour, gens de couleur libres, whose father, by all accounts was white, letting his "son" buy his freedom. His total worth, or what was paid for his manumission was 1500 dollars, which in the 19$^{th}$ century was quite a sum. Sarah took to marriage, happily learning to make maque choux and jambalaya for her husband. There was an ever-ready supply of chicken, eggs, and pork, not to mention the occasional sweets, praline pecans, and sugar, from locals bartering for her husband's services.

## VI.

**Jim Crow Laws:** Birthed in 1876, to uphold the premise of separate but equal. The one-drop rule during the turn of the century was made famous, designating blacks based on minimal African blood.

This was a new war. A stealthy creeping war that slithered across dark wetlands like water moccasins blended in the ripples. One bite, one drop and families were torn apart. The Code Noir forgotten, as new Protestants and hierarchies of colour tumbled and jumbled across a land— where the colour line had been fuzzy at best. Passé blanc was a way to survival. Keeping eyes down cast, crossing the street to avoid dark skinned cousins and chance meetings— Training the tongue to forget Halito and Bonswa, while tripping over square un-romantic phrasings that left lips dry and parched with wanting the humid heat of a language that revealed more than one drop... Mulâtre...Indígena.

Sarah's daughters married, raising children. They were fair skinned and hazel eyed. Her sons, moreno, nègre— They were separate but equal, taking jobs as field hands, and in domestic servitude—They are now lost to the descendants of her daughters.

## VII.

**métis:** [mā-'tē(s)] plural mé·tis \-'tē(s), -'tēz\. Etymology: French, from Late Latin mixticius mixed — see mestizo.
1. A person of mixed blood.
2. The offspring of an American Indian and a person of European Ancestry.

The word Métis comes from the Latin "miscere" or "mixticius," meaning to mix. The word has been used in French speaking colonies to describe the children of Indian women and French men. In Greek mythology Métis was a Titan, mother of Athena, and patron of crafting and weaving skills. Métis in Greek was also the everyday word for combined wisdom and cunning, and the origin of weaving— Métis, to weave, to create, a new race, a people.

## VIII.

The Rabbit's have a long genealogy. Chukfi remembers the stories of his great grandmother, and their emergence from Nanih Waiya. His cuz, Brier, made a name for himself, even got his own book. But Chukfi, he wanted nothing to do with Brier. Chukfi tricked a wolf, and Brier a fox. Chukfi's mother wove baskets of river cane or pine needles, and Brier's mother wove baskets of sweetgrass. Chukfi, well he taught his daughters about Christ in Baptist churches, and Brier, well his kids knelt reciting the rosary. Cuzins separated by colour and boxes, and those moved, those left behind, and those too dark to admit they were kin... Colour changes the narrative again, in Lwizyàn.

No space for Indian, got to pick a side. Misbegotten laws lead to passing, cause there was no box for Louisiana Choctaws, and her brother had left to Oklahoma, driven by the promise of land under Dawes. So Edna gave her son her father's club, skull cracker, carved with symbols of the whirlwind, spirals, and Bear Chief. A remembrance of the time before, even though she made sure they wrote "White" on his certificate of birth. But her son, his eye was caught by the decedents of Brier Rabbit, by way of Cane River, the daughters and granddaughters of women with names like Jemima, Maymae, Ingababo, and Apolonia with fancy

French surnames. However, Edna could not deny the beauty of her grandchildren, taking them to dig sassafras and witch-hazel, reading to them from the bible, and singing them a song for crawdad.

## IX.
**misbegotten** [misbə'gätn]
*adj*
    1. unlawfully obtained misbegotten gains
    2. of, or relating to, or being a child or children born to unmarried parents.
    3. badly conceived, planned, or designed a misbegotten scheme.
    4. also misbegot [misbə'gätn] *Literary and dialect* illegitimate; bastard

I named my child Misbegot. She is after all, the bastard child of multigenerational mestizos, métis and griffes. Who is she? Olive skinned, green-eyed child whose features at once harken the rolling hills of Ireland and the crisp hills of Scotland, bayous and palms of Gulf Coast Southern Indians, the dry heat of Southern border towns, the shores of West Africa, the windy high plains of Saskatchewan and Alberta First Nations, and pacific central humidity of Nahuatl peoples? Sitting on the patio in the humid southern heat, I rock her slowly against my breast, singing names, calling upon ancestors to light the thread of her life woven into a cast net, of red, black, and white– Rocking, we sing the cosmos, our words like a net drawing down stars whose light greeted our ancestors as they crossed borders, racial divides, ignoring misbegotten laws of miscegenation in favor of survival...

### Cane River Tanka II

Sister-cuzin's porch
      mosquitoes buzz in humid
afternoon dusk of
      pearlescent fog. Our murmurs
          mingle with ancestors, float

**Prayer for Sinners**

I can teach the art of silence
        suckled from elongated chapped nipples
and lips bit split bloody

Lose individuality of fingerprints
        to repetition of rosary
Hail Mary full of grace
        what happened to our blessed wombs?

Hiding in cane breaks
secrets whisper blood down thighs
language of fists and curses

Learn to weave rivercane
        so it spills entrails like alligator's
split belly carry home teeth and toes
        Remember I survived

Cover cracked mirrors
        Kneel as in mass light fire to toughened souls
of my feet slash and burn

        Holy Mary, Mother of God
        who labeled us sinners?

## How Turtle Begins to Relearn her Language
### (broken shell & broken phrases)

| | |
|---|---|
| Anumpa nan anoli sabvnna. | I want to tell a story. |
| Bok chitto a yvy pvlhki hosh yanvlli. | The water is flowing fast to the ocean. |
| Luksi insht aⁿya shali chukka | Turtle carry the home. |
| Hatchotakni insht aⁿya shali yakni | Sea Turtle carry the land. |
| Hatchotakni insht aⁿya shali pvt Okla | Sea Turtle carry the People. |
| Yakni isht ikhana | The land is record keeper. |
| Okla isht ikhana | The People are record keeper. |
| | |
| Binolhichi. | Colonization. |
| | |
| Lokaffit isht ia. | Recovery. |
| | |
| Luksi insht aⁿya shali chukka | Turtle carry the home. |
| Hatchotakni insht aⁿya shali yakni | Sea Turtle carry the land. |
| Hatchotakni insht aⁿya shali pvt Okla | Sea Turtle carry the People. |
| Bok chitto a yvy pvlhki hosh yanvlli. | The water is flowing fast to the ocean. |

## Apocryphal Blues[vi]

Five years gone absence of touch
wears down spirit like rock in water
tumbles angles of heart turn jagged and hollow.
Water has left my body
leaves me unbalanced
                I list left wards.

*Our Lady of Prompt Succor against lightning and tempest, pray for us.*
*Our Lady of Prompt Succor against destruction by flood, pray for us.*

When Turtle broke her shell
She sang, calling ants who shaking
came to sing her back together.
But my voice is broken, unlike this shell,
no song to call and response
                me whole.

*my attachment to my native land was strong–*
*that cord is now broken.*

Who is there to keep me safe,
cover me when bombs come, trace tracks
of my scars internal or external, still pulsing,
raise keloids can't stop growing. Whose fingertips
will apply pressure when scars itch, threaten to
burst open from pulse of blood seeking escape.
We leak like sap down trees into red soil,
I wonder is that how red dirt
                becomes red.

*Here is the land of our progenitors, and here are*
*their bones; they left them as a sacred deposit.*

You anoint, attach wings, sing on high,
and lay claim to celestial knowledge that
somehow I am apocryphal in the scripted

scroll you call sacred. That I might carve
a little space for myself in the footnotes a blip
      of anarchy in your erasure.

*Our Lady of Prompt Succor against the enemies of our country, pray for us.*
*Our Lady of Prompt Succor in time of war, pray for us.*

## II. Uncle Jim Two-Steps
"Indians of the nation, the wild, wild creation. We won't
bow down, down on the ground"
— Danny Barker and The Wild Tchoupitoulas, "Indian Red"

# Historical Codes and Observations II: A Found Poem[vii]

District of the Attakapas received its name
from Attakapas Indians
a ~~fierce~~ (resilient) tribe
that ~~inhabited~~ (inhabits)
the area ~~before~~ (despite)
the coming of the white man.

1739 De Nouaille described ~~Apappapas~~ Atakapas,
who resided on seashore of Louisiana
live(ing) mostly on fish. According to ~~tradition~~
(***rumors based on white colonial racism***)
these Indians were "cannibals."

> ~~We~~ (Wypipo) forbid slaves
> to carry offensive weapons or heavy sticks,
> under the penalty of being whipped

(***According to the ramblins of an elderly racially biased white man***):
Avoyels were captured and "made good eating."
Storm of 1810 was disastrous on Gulf
bodies of shipwrecked sailors
washed ashore near Calcasieu.
Bodies were roasted in a pit but
shaman gave it that if the Atakapa
ate flesh of white men their
skin would become spotty
(Wypipo- *not* the other white meat).

> ~~We~~ (Wypipo) declare slaves
> can have no right to property
> all that they acquire shall be
> the full property of their masters.

1811, one year before Louisiana became a state

            Council decreed:
"County of Attakapas
            shall be divided into
Parish of St Martin
Parish of St. Mary."

## Poème pour Tonton Jim

"In appearance, manner, and form she is not 'black'; her blackness must be written upon her... Indeed, it is the purpose of the octoroon to pose (as) the problem of racial discernment" (107).
—Sybil Kein, *Creole: the History and Legacy of Louisiana's Free People of Colour.*

This is a poem for Uncle Jim
Who *made love* to me Sundays after church.
After church called it
        Making love—
His hand over my mouth.
        Over my mouth,
                His hand after church.

Lips blushed first from petal pink
To crimson hush, turning purple under
Heavy, thin-fingered white blue marbled hand—
Til bottom lip split like overripe plums hitting
Red dirt soil in too soon summer.
        Til I am split overripe plum.

Blushing first time he told me to
Call him,
        Call him Tonton Jim.
Making relations with a white man,
Law making man, traveling man, whose
Tobacco spit hits red dirt soil.
        Who hits red dirt soil
              Who hit red.

Uncle Jim
Used to wave to me
Calling me to his side when he saw
Me walking down the street.
His favorite niece,
"Petite nièce pale."

His *favorite*, as fairly fetching as any
Octoroon in Mahogany Hall— dark hair
Pinned high, face protected under wide brim
Hat— So as not to yellow my slightly
Tea stained porcelain complexion.

Uncle Jim
Kept the line taunt.
Taunt as his hands over my breasts
Which he coveted—
For their fullness, their paleness,
Their secret forbidden history.
       My breasts,
              Over my breasts *his hands*
       Keeping the line taunt.

Uncle Jim
Refused to acknowledge my sister,
"La jeune fille noire—L'Indien, sauvage."
She, who resembled too much,
Our dark Chahta grandmother—
Too much remembrance of
West Africa in Creole
Blood of our Mother
Femme de couleur libres.

Uncle Jim
Pretended I was abandoned
Like his own children left wandering
Along Calcasieu and Red Rivers...
Their dark mothers silent as bayou waters
From too much
       too much, too much...
       Tonton Jim.

## Cathoindian
*for Carrie*

I am lighting candles to St. Kateri.

I am burning sweetgrass and cedar.

I am praying to Our Lady of Prompt Succor.

While offering tobacco by the river.

## Levee Womb Blues[viii]

I named for fallin water's mindful balance.
    *If it keeps on raining the levee goin ta break*
Rivers rising like his hand up my skirt, nails welting flesh,
Raises keloid banks like bodies, death memory ridges.

    *If it keeps on raining the levee goin ta break*
Rollin waves of music slappin flesh, ripplin stories
Raises keloid banks like bodies, death memory ridges,
Gripped by his tumble n' thrust ridin my broken bruises.

Rollin waves of music slappin flesh, ripples stories.
Whisperin prayers to Sinti lapitta and Damballah
Gripped by his tumble n' thrust ridin my broken bruises.
    *Cryin won't help you prayin won't do no good*

Whisperin prayers to Sinti lapitta and Damballah,
Womb walls break tumblin' down scarlet water
    *Cryin won't help you prayin won't do no good.*
Safety of water washin away 'nother man's sins.

Womb walls break tumblin' down scarlet water
White sins worked on red-black body leavin blues.
Safety of water washin away 'nother man's sins.
    *Got wha'it takes make a bayou gal leave her home.*

White sins worked on red-black body leavin blues
Rivers rising like his hand up my skirt, nails welting flesh
    *Got wha'it takes make a bayou gal leave her home.*
I still named for fallin water's, mindful balance.

## Chitlins no More

Lard, fat back, slaughter house, smoke house
tell ya what— its all goot here, hog fry, bacon,
salt pork, everything tastes better with shukha!

Don't bring me no greens without hocks,
bacon, some bell pepper, and cayenne!
Now daddy can throw down, bébé sis too,
I make a smothered pork chop have ya slap
ya mama fo' second helping, that's right,
everthin tastes better with shukha!

Cracklin on grits and on fried catfish,
Banaha with salt pork and poke salad.
we have a love affair goin on here
and ya'll need to understand this relationship
outlasted many a man, cause shukha is stayin—
it puts flava in the pot *and* greases the pan.

From the rooter to the tooter they say
but one cut o'meat I don't eat. Once ya
clean your share of chitlins—
I'm done, put that hose where no sun shines
I draw the line— Chitlins no more...

Lard, fat back, slaughter house, smoke house
tell ya what— its all goot here, hog fry, bacon,
salt pork, everything tastes better with shukha!

But once ya put that hose where no sun shines
I draw the line— Chitlins no more...
Now pass the smother'd chops fo' I slap ya mama!

## Opelousas, September 28 1868

**I.**
Early ripples from Shreveport
reach St. Landry parish. This state
floats on water; we are constantly
ebbing and flowing, forever feeling
repercussions of stones thrown in
estuaries and Gulf.

*Sometimes I feel*
*like a motherless child*[ix]

News carried on breeze, whispered
in moss, drips language down into soil
then creeps into feet creates an intimacy
in our flesh, a knowing of violence to come.
Opelousas' turn, Bossier City bubbling
wait, (Colfax at ready).

**II.**
Bentley broken for writing
what they were promised:[x]
To sign their names,
make them count— freed
slaves to gens de couleur libres.
But new hurricane come, rising
white capped hostile takeover.

*Sometimes I feel*
*like a motherless child*

There are no shades of gray,
no red to choose. It is black
or white. Welcome the new
south, the promised land—
United we stand.

**III.**
Bentley busted white body
heading north homeward—
our tan, olive, brown, black,
red, highyella, coloured
selves scattered to swaps in
shuffle snake survivals.

*Sometimes I feel*
*like I'm almos' gone*

Seymour Knight's bullets
beat bodies, blowing holes
in coloured flesh size of
pallid camellia flowers.

**IV.**
This is a hostile takeover
we have no recourse in the
land of cotton & cane.
Promise of milk and honey
ripples away like cottonmouth
trail in murky bayou water.

*Sometimes I feel*
 *like I'm almos' gone*

Our milk is that from our mothers.
Our honey stolen from the comb.
But, still it's a hostile takeover, it is
not our fate to smell the magnolia trees,
but bruise their blossoms as we swing.

## Love Song for Paracolonial Occupation

I know this groove: miscegenation beatbox mix born in bayou underground, refined by muscle shoals "Alabama Motown"– driven by sugarcane, Irish fiddlers, cotton-stepped Go down Moses field gospels, and call & response stomp songs. This is the tune I am bent over to, legs kicked apart, hips set to bump-n-grind in time as I release my miscegenation méstiza blues. A wailin howl– part Buffy, part Billie, and part Lila. Thighs drippin blood as my eyes pop hemorrhaging: paracolonial witness, paracolonial witness. Parts of body swell from my ankles to my wrists. My face burned with your brand. I watch my hair falling, cells in my own body turn on my organs and lupus "cures" you pump into me are pharmaceutical seeds. Their side effects planting flags where your semen could not travel, into twist and turn of dna, corrupting synapses that whisper in languages you don't understand; Ahnit: Ohoyo Tvshka, Ohoyo Creole, Ohoyo Bayuk. And our land América Indígena from South to North, Mapuche to the Iñupiat we are marked: certified occupied. I feel my body breaking, as you ride my rung out hips your seed leaking with my blood and I keep singin this song just for you– We never forget, never surrender
    My eyes have seen, my spirit remains: paracolonial witness,
              paracolonial witness.
                    Unoccupy me.

# Footnotes on Decoding Louisiana Indigenous & Racial Subtexts
(or the things left unsaid)

Cajun[1]
Creole[2]
Indian[3]
Redbone[4]
Swamp Injun[5]

Highyella[6]
Blindian[7]
French Creole[8]
White[9]
Disenfranchised Native[10]

---

[1] Historically poorer and white, and yeah In'din. There's a time folks t'wast always ok wit it but we's gotten more ok wit it. (But still aint no ways there was a tar baby).

[2] We are Indigenous to this here land, African, Indian, French, and Spanish. Some say they more black, some more white, some more Indian, but we's Creole, an Indigenous American Southern Latinidad Culture, not a colour, not a race.

[3] We are *The People Who Stayed*. When you're ready to deal with that I'll tell you the rest...

[4] We are the POC future with a rich history...hello, AfroNDNCaucasian with a sprinkling of other. Culturally bayou rural.

[5] Not all Indians live in Teepees and eat buffalo genius... have some gumbo and banaha.

[6] Ya didn't realize I was black did ya?

[7] Black and Indian, welcome to Louisiana. Atakapa-Ishak, Houma, Bayougoula, Apalachee, yah dey's mixed with us. Can't find the right box?

[8] I am a Proud "White" Creole, I am sure my ancestors are directly from France... I am sure.... very...well, very sure.

[9] My ancestors are relatively new to Louisiana.

[10] Non- enrollable in a Louisiana Tribe due to relocation or politics. Recognition is awesome for those of whose parents left for relocation or employment. Ask about my language, community, landbase, and culture? Let the authenticity litmus-test begin!

## Poem for Mary Edmonia Lewis (1844-1907)

In you I see reflection
wildfire temperament unrelenting
Afro-Caribbean-Indian sister
to North of me.

Marble organic images emerge
smooth except occasional rough planes and
angles belling white stone with echo
of faces in colour, from Minnehaha to Hiawatha.

Twist and turn of Roman gods
bend to your Red-Black hands,
the excess chiseled away, like
giving up memories of rumor and
nighttime mob Oberlin, Ohio beatings.

Here on Gulf to Red River,
I am your likeness, you my mirror
in fire, rather than water, burned
to darker ash, as I become muted in
widening ripples of song displaced
against Cane River's mirrored surface.

## Dr. Frankenstein and the BIA

Victor got a new job
the perfect gig,
all the parts he wants—
The BIA and Identity police
need his expertise
tacking dead NDN bits together
to prove mixedbloods
can't sustainably be

That ancestry doesn't exist—
So they are told from experts on high,
state tribes are lies and culture
can't be inherited or persistent
in bodies like thine.
Well there's too damn many mixedbloods,
too many multicoloured NDNs,
too many Creoles, Latinos, Méstizos to see.

Dr. Frankenstein raided,
the Smithsonian, some NDN graves,
& don't forget that dna they keep on hand
(real double helix of the aboriginal 'merican)

He took scraps and bits,
pair o'Creole hips and legs,
Scottish neck, organs of Ishak,
body of Chahta & shoulders of Settler,
Skin of Ireland, wrists of a Creek,
Latinidad lips and Freedmen feet.
Found himself some miscellaneous
Louisiana folxs' fingers, toes, & Welsh nose.
Got himself a fine pair of unknown
arms & haunted eyes. Sewed on a
North of 49 métis head & taught it to speak.

He sewed & tacked,

Glued and baked—
Put his mixedblood under
lighting till it sat up and spake.
Then charge went dead—
& off flopped that wobbly mixed-up head.

So today I got the news—
Ain't no mixedbloods,
the race can't survive—
in fact Dr. Frankenstein knows
NDNs of all kinds are on the demise.

## Love Poem for Jim Crow

Sultry southern heat keeps our blood and our secrets deep.
We learn silence at foot of beds like prayers we kneel—
for loving and absolution, both leaving something to weep.

The dirt here is red from blood and peoples we seep.
Memories encroach as cawing corvid's pecking peel
sultry southern heat keeps our blood and our secrets deep.

Uncle Jim came, Northern dandy, with his fine new line to keep
stirrin' whispers, negated our relations, uncovered secrets to deal
for loving and absolution, both leaving something to weep.

Traipsing in fear and in superior belief some followed like sheep
keepin' time on'da side with my dark grandmothers, kept in heel.
Sultry southern heat keeps our blood and our secrets deep.

The deeper the line cuts into soft flesh the more Jim would creep
quietly into beds of la jeune fille sauvage seeking something real
for loving and absolution, both leaving something to weep.

I am love poem left by Jim Crow— price of writing steep,
words carved on flesh turned keloid never truly heal.
Sultry southern heat keeps our blood and our secrets deep,
for loving and absolution, both leaving something to weep.

### Mixedblood Girls I (who've dated FBIs)

Let this settle:
Problem ain't your blood quantum,
your enrollment or lack of CDIB.
It has nuttin ta do wit ya being rez,
urban, or country, whether ya be
brown, black, highyella, or melanin
challenged.

But he gonna tell ya it is.
And if'n he don't some bro,
sis, or cuz, will. Your place was predetermined
the minute your non Hollywood NDN lookin
ass stepped into his world. Hell, you might be ¾,
even full, but from the wrong side of I-35
or a terminated or state tribe. You just don't look
the part, speak their language, or perhaps you're a
5-Civ in a high-plains or SW ho-down.
Your role was cast. You're the
mixedblood patsy.

And should your relationship break,
cuz you're too sober, or too educated,
or too traditional, or frankly not mixed enuff,
or not'a wannabe, to *believe* the steaming pile o'
BS he claims as tradition to keep you *down*,
sayin what you know, learned, how you was
raised was wrong... don't you dare let that bro,
or cuz, who been stiffin at your door take you out.
Cuz mixedblood patsy, you're gonna be the
not really NDN slut.

Dating Indigy style:
We put the "fun
in dysfunctional."

### Going Home
*for sisters Tee, & Carrie*

I come from water driven up from Gulf into
tributaries like arteries of a delta Mother whose scares
are keloid Red-Black as my own double helix.
My heart pumps this blood— works it like a tide
ebbing in and out.

Driving to Louisiana homelands salt in air
thickens sky turns deeper shade of blue.
I watch for small blue herons, the eternal white of egret,
like a fresh laundered shirt, or a soul free of sin.

Closer I move to delta land, rivers bisect paths
and wading birds surround territories
in simple acts of resistance, like Louisiana's
peoples themselves— refusing removal from
encroaching misnomer "civilization."

There is a sacredness to waterbirds; wading birds,
plovers, cranes, water turkeys. They seem to
operate in half Mvskogean half Southern black
folk religion—They go to water.

Without water we are out of balance.
I have been splayed and torn,
blood broken to bruises without water
to wash healing onto beaten skin.
Acts of reinscription to demarcations of savage
are painful. I reinscribe what it means to
resist through
GRACE.

Going home means going to water.
Cane River, Red River, Spring Bayou,
Calcasieu, Bayou Teche, Gulf of Mexico.
Each spot story. Water is fluid,

gives birth, winds like a woman's
body, and shelters life.

Wade in water
wash weary soul.
Go to water,
cleanse and pray.

Home to Louisiana
sister and her children beside us—
we stop at Cane River.
Cedar, tobacco fall to red
muddy veins. Looking across
river cane break boasts pair
of egrets keeping vigil—
we offer up prayer.
All we remember,
all that we are, from
shame to survival,
to pride and this next
generation balanced on our hips.

### III. A'Capella Rattle Songs
"Okla e maya momakma.../
Yakni i natanna ibachvffa hosh okla
il ilai achonli tuk
Hapi fiopa ya shotik chinto okla
il itibani tuk"
— Samantha Crain "We Remain"

# Removals and Relocations[xi]

An Act to provide for an ~~exchange~~ STEALING of lands from **Indians** And for their ~~removal~~ west of the river Mississippi. It shall be lawful for the President of the United States to (Encourage **Indians** to abandon hunting, for raising stock, agriculture and domestic manufacture prove to themselves that less **land** and labor will maintain them. ~~This is better than in their former mode of living~~.)

Lawful for the President to exchange any or all of such districts, so to be laid off and described, with any **tribe** or **nation** within the limits of any of the states or *territories*, and with which the United States have existing **treaties**, for the whole or any part or portion of the <u>territory claimed and occupied by such</u> **tribe** or **nation**, within the bounds of any one or more of the states or *territories*, where the <u>land claimed and occupied by the</u> **Indians**, is owned by the United States, or the United States are bound to the state within which it lies to ~~extinguish the Indian~~ claim thereto. (To multiply trading houses among them, and place within their reach those things which will contribute more to their domestic comfort, than the possession of extensive, but uncultivated wilds.)

It shall be lawful for the President to assure the **tribe** or **nation** the United States will **forever secure** and **guaranty** to them and their heirs or successors ~~the country~~ (**Indian Territory**) so exchanged with them provided always
such **lands** shall revert to the United States
if the ~~Indians become extinct or abandon the same~~
(At the whim of settler governments).

47

## Cartography: Self Help
*For Papa, Granddaddy and Grandmother*

Traveling synapses languages
mingle across time and tribe
into pidgins recognizable only
by familial blood.

Epidermis, to keloids, varicose veins,
scabs partially healed and leaking gashes,
open spread-eagle torn, seeping cries
while I remain silent eyes on ceiling—

This wound is mine, but I am not
first to take it, to leave blood on
sheets, or page, our scars read like
frictions of fiction in survivals.

Terrains are mapped in self-exploration.
This old scar was not mine, came from
nun at Youllville, ripped deeper in Edmonton and
St. Albert's, left my Papa bleeding. Took to flame
cauterized himself in drink and forgetting.
Then passed the scars to mom, then me and sister.

A family tree worked by exacto knife
of Southern racism. Tough skin heals
small tributaries. They line my back working
their way raised pulsing rivers seeking to
break seal of skin flow to great Gulf
water, the source mother, salt healer. Passed
by my father, from his father and mother.

Belonging to this genealogy means
an obsession with the topography of pain.

**Dust Bowl Blues**
*for Grandmother & big sis JCM*

Black thorn pierce naked foot
               bleed red
        overhead black crow blue tinged wings
                 trip on broken branch
Broken branch no spring bud magnolias
               to bruise broken in Billie's hair
      broken notes slip past lips
              trembling like timpani

Trembling timpani rumble call
              thunder come down memory
      like sermon brimstone trembling
              dredge lake sludge corpse rotting
    this is what we buried

Broken branch trembling like timpani
              under wary perched black crow
        tinged blue as bruise and this black thorn
            bleeds red on
    Oklahoma dust

## Tiny Tots

July after sundown
humid Oklahoma heat—
But the *wind comes
sweeping down the plain*[xii].
Just enough to abate sticky
necks of Indians, whispering hair
in shades from black to brown,
even some honey-headed.

July in Oklahoma means
powwow, forty-nine, sis, bro and kids
piled high, dogs and cooler, blankets
regalia, slim jims and root beer.
Cuz if ya aint dancin
you holdin the baby on your hip
bouncin up and down, on balls of your
feet. Don't matter how ample your belly
or hips be, drum and honor beats
thrum into earth and up into your
toes, setting body into
remembrance of motion—
Dancin, on the sideline.

In circle tiny tots mingle their jingles
grapple their little mocs to grass dance—
trying to keep eyes on oversized
beads flyin, like sparkling sequins
in dance circle lights.
Fluttering shawls and aprons merging
green, fuchsia, turquoise blurring in
a flurry of watercolour motion.
Chubby hands lunging...

Candy Dance.

**Tongue**

I dreamed tongues tangled in sensuous sashay,
keep time to blood pumped blues in slide—
Sprits that move against time worn edges of day.

As sun rose lips broke trip-hop into allegro fray
rolling sucking, tremble tips where our promises hide.
I dreamed tongues tangled in sensuous sashay.

Kneel in reverence, work in rhythm, bodies that pray
these soul ached notes escape and like doves' wings glide—
Sprits that move against time worn edges of day.

Outside dewdrops glisten opulence where they lay
inside cedar and magnolia tinged musks lift and collide.
I dreamed tongues tangled in sensuous sashay.

Crescendos build wailings in key of E strange cachet
swollen lips, and limbs like willows weep limp outside—
Sprits that move against time worn edges of day.

Mouths part like seas and words finally give way
as heart drummed stomped tunes quietly subside—
I dreamed tongues tangled in sensuous sashay.
Like Sprits move against time worn edges of day.

**Mixedblood Girls II**

Mixedblood girls who date
                      white boys are traitors to their race
                                  cuz' "girl don't you know
you're supposed to up your blood quantum?"


Mixedblood Girls who date
                      black guys isolate family
                                    cuz don't you
know grandma & grandpa spent a lifetime
                      pretndin they "really weren't them
                                    Freedmen folk."
Keepin' family separated. Cuz there's more than one kind of rez.

Mixedblood girls who date
                      other mixedblood girls learn to keep
                                    their faces up,
wear their tattoos like shawls of tradition, & teach other
                      mixedblood girls songs of their
                                    grandmothers
full, throaty, and rich with defiance of
              being mixedblood girls
                    who didn't claim to be anything else.

# Testimony: A Song[xiii]
*For the Mvskoke Divas*

**I.**
I traversed my mother's birth canal, leaving the knowledge of certainty
and entering a world of false doors and broken windows.

At birth we know secrets of the universe—the next day answers are erased,
leaving us only memory of blood—song with muted words.

We pray to and dream of a god that weaves a hoyv, calls the winds sons
and suckles us with rains brought on feathered serpent wings.

We are placed like drops of dew on web of cosmos.

This our memory, our blood, Our Grandmother.

**II.**
In our brother's bundle are thirteen wampums. We pray with him
in thanks of them each night. The spirits of the dead are poles
sent down river—free to travel wherever thought takes them.

We dare not speak their names and disrupt them on their journey.

**III.**
Obsidian night where we first lived inside belly of Mother Earth
sings song known in every vein of my sisters' blood. We've come
for sayvtketv. Shuffling feet tied to locv.

**IV.**
Broken words and cracked stones, small white smooth little eggs
of tribal memory, strung on sinew and worn about our throats.
Whispering in the hollow between neck and collar—whispers to blood—
       To you who spirits dwell and abide in the North

grant us good dreams.
To you who spirits dwell and abide in the West
show us the path so we may seek wisdom.
To you who spirits dwell and abide in the South
let our words be both spiritual and practical.
To you who spirits dwell and abide in the East
let us care for those not strong enough to care for themselves.

Make game plentiful, corn abundant, and our medicines strong
for all our people.

**Fish Guts**
*for Dad & bébé sis*

Dad's stringer strung with Spanish mackerel,
Reds, and Speckled Trout could have been a

perfectly carved abalone necklace or a string
of pearls way bébé sis's eyes light up. Running

to front porch chubby tan bare toddler feet, sagging
terrycloth clad bottom, and drooping cerulean blue

bikini top, her gray eyes sparkle like raindrops on
concrete in her bronze face as Tee runs to meet the

evening catch. Later in back yard on concrete
slab we call a patio limp wet bodies slide off blue

rope and steel needle onto newspaper. Hitting black
white print. Tee grabs each cold slick full scaly body

and raising them to her rosebud lips kisses round fish
eyes: "mmm mmm yummy!" This is their ritual before

butter knife sheds scales of their opalescence. Rush of
garden hose assisting on back porch, shimmering small

flat rainbows glittering in green grass and sand patches.
Before blade slides from vent under tail to head, then under

gills to tail filleting strips of pale pink flesh. Before pink,
gray, and red guts and row spill slimy ooze onto day old

newspaper that will find its way to the trash
or tomorrow's chum bucket.

This is their ritual.
Welcoming home the evening catch.

## Oklahoma Ghazal

A restaurant on outskirts of Norman, Indian women are laughing in Oklahoma.
Wide lush lips splitting over white squared teeth in round faces in Oklahoma.

Eyes turn crinkles over broad cheekbones, dimple dipped full cheeks— canyons of story
Indian women laughing in shades of sassafras bark to the pale golden sky in Oklahoma.

Northside of OKC children huddle under a Pendleton giggling away their secrets.
Their arms, legs, a tangle of tree limbs, their bodies rooted to this soil in Oklahoma.

Child laughter crow-hops across the house to the lone adult sitting silent in darkness—
An air conditioner whirrs to life— she passing her tongue over broken front tooth in Oklahoma.

Cool air rushes to warm skin but the smell of outside lingers on hair and clothes something—
Spicy like green onion, the faint smell of Gulf salt, and the sweetness of red dirt in Oklahoma.

# Down by the River[xiv]

You can find me by banks of the river
my hands buried in water
Down bayou side on banks that open and crack
Raise my song open my veins tryin
to call up bones of my sisters
sing red toned blues to call them back

*In my time of dying, want nobody to mourn*
*All I want is for you take my body home*

I've preached these blues where we go to pray
down by okhina putting up tobacco, cedar, sage
Made offerings of tequila, banaha, marq choux
Left yellowed pictures scrapes of poems in brack water
I have offered my blood carrying three races
sung my voice raw bloody lipped prayers
for the holy, prayers for the lonely
A psalm by the water as it ebbs and flows

*In my time of dying, want nobody to mourn*
*All I want is for you take my body home*

Taught my spirit to levitate
ate suko and anhipon
Purified myself with end of sharpen cane
Yet I stand lonely and now
this body slipped its soil
trying to paddle up stream

*In my time of dying, want nobody to mourn*
*All I want is for you take my body home*
      *take my body home*

## Hugs and kisses/Besos y abrazos

I learned touch of a soft tongue
your firm lips meshed to mine
Toned torso and firm breasts
merge and rock against swell
Of my belly weight of my breasts

I learned to seek sweet musk and
salt between brown thighs
Forgetting to feel shame in size
of my body embracing
ways you made me weep for you

I learned truth of living
the in-between, neither red nor white
black nor red, straight or gay
strong or soft,
power and powerless

We gloss each other's
lips with dew staccato sing
down stars that witnessed
the birth of our ancestors
the creation of our race

The testament
of in between

Aprendí el toque de una lengua suave
tus labios firmes se enredaron con los míos
Torso tonificado y senos firmes
fusionar y rockear contra el oleaje
De mi vientre peso de mis senos

Aprendí a buscar almizcle dulce y
sal entre muslos marrones
Olvidando sentir vergüenza en tamaño
de mi cuerpo abrazando
maneras en las que me hiciste llorar por ti

Aprendi la verdad de vivir
la intermedia, ni rojo ni blanco
negro ni rojo, heterosexual o gay
fuerte o suave
poder y sin poder

Nos damos brillo el uno al otro
labios con rocío staccato cantar
abajo estrellas que presenciaron
el nacimiento de nuestros antepasados
la creación de nuestra raza.

El testamento
de entre

## Shaking Lodge

Regret is a religion
lives under the skin
parasite

Like a burned braid
unraveled this
thunderclap revelation
torn prayer smoke
vibration slipped
smoke from lips

I lost the shape
of breasts belly thighs
This body when you ceased
to tracing me against your
calloused hands at night

We speak a language
made of water in a
land turned to sand
That this cedar could
Call them back
Call them back
Call me back
from where we went
when the darkness came
When your darkness came

I see you burrow
through epidermis lay roots
like arteries map and trap
cells of intent vibrate through
my cellulite and muscle

make me a shaking lodge

### Rising Sun[xv]

That there was a black woman
                              and a French man.
That there was an Indian woman
                              and a French man.
That there was an Indian man
                              and an African-Spanish woman.
That there is more than one
      more than one
            more than one
                  more than one
                        in your skin.

Across Pearl River to Terrebonne
from Point Coupee to New Orleans

                *There is a house in New Orleans*

That my breasts hang heavy in memory
having suckled children
      born along Cane River
            carried along Calcasieu
                  whose little bodies were bathed in Spring Bayou.

Can you feel the water in your skin?
Can you hear our morning prayers?

                      *Call to the rising sun*

In Opelousas you shot and hung us.
At Red River Indian Agency you starved us.
In Natchitoches and Marksville you took us
to wife as if marriage vows and census would erase us.

                 *Spent my life in sheer misery*

But their blood is my blood

       is my blood
            is my blood
                 is our blood
and our prayers in the morning still go to the

               *Rising Sun*

### IV. Zydeco Round Dances
"I rule the bayou land... I got my gris-gris dust, my mojo hand."
— Coco Robicheaux "Louisiana Medicine Man"

Removals and Relocations II [xvi]

>To make **Indians** within territorial limits of the United States **subject to the same laws** and **entitled to the same privileges and responsibilities:**

all persons similarly situated, **being of Choctaw and Chickasaw descent and blood,** and **members of the Choctaw and Chickasaw tribes or communities** of Indians, and who were before the Commission to the Five Civilized Tribes under the provisions of the Act approved June 28, 1898

>That petitioner was a citizen of the United States and **a resident** of the state **of Louisiana,** of **mixed descent,** the mixture of coloured blood was not discernible in him, and that he **was entitled to every recognition, right, privilege, and immunity** secured to the citizens of the United States of the white race by its constitution and laws

In order to ~~help~~ adult Indians who reside on or near Indian reservations to ~~obtain reasonable and satisfactory employment,~~ the Secretary of the Interior is authorized to undertake a program of ~~vocational training~~. Indians who are not less than eighteen and not more than thirty-five years of age and who reside on or near an Indian reservation, and the program shall be conducted under such rules and regulations as the Secretary may prescribe.

>While we think the enforced separation of the races, as applied to the internal commerce of the State, neither abridges the privileges or immunities of the coloured man, deprives him of his property without due process of law, nor denies him the equal protection of the laws within the meaning of the Fourteenth Amendment— We uphold ~~equal~~ but separate accommodations for the white, and coloured, races.

Directed the Commission to make "correct rolls" of the Choctaw and Chickasaw **FREEDMEN** entitled to any rights or benefits under the treaty of 1866, and their descendants thereafter born Provided always

That such lands shall revert to the United States, if the Indians become extinct, or abandon the same.

## Issish/San

Raucous beating blood
Chew through sinewy meat
on wrists to bleed
out noise.
>San raucous bat
>Moulen nan vyann dezole
>sou ponyèt yo senyen
>soti bri.

How many voices
scream through arteries
where ghosts move, sliding
between muscle and bone?
>Konbyen vwa
>rele atravè atè yo
>kote fantom deplase, glisman
>ant misk ak zo?

Successions of women,
before me—
memory keepers.
>Siksesyon nan fanm,
>devan mwen—
>gadè memwa yo.

Carrying corpses against their bruised breasts
their hips still crack, crack, crack—
like a whip, like a gun, like swinging hand on flesh.
>Pote kadav yo kont pwent panche yo
>ranch yo toujou krak, krak, krak-
>tankou yon fwèt, tankou yon zam,
>tankou men balanse sou vyann.

At night, I am tormented. My spirit pulled like puppet on strings so there is no will or fight. Learn to be slack-jawed,

doe-eyed, empty-headed
> Lannwit, mwen soufri anpil. Lespri mwen rale tankou
> mannken sou strings se konsa
> pa gen okenn volonte oswa goumen.
> Aprann yo dwe kansè machwè, je sèf, tèt vid

That's a good little girl. That's a good little girl.
> Sa se yon bon ti fi. Sa se yon bon ti fi.

In morning, I take manicure scissors
split my tongue to better speak
two languages without upsetting
balance of my mouth.
> Nan maten, mwen pran sizo manukur
> separe lang mwen an pi byen pale
> de lang san yo pa boulvèsan
> balans nan bouch mwen.

I catch the blood from my tongue
in a cup to paint my eyelids, lips, and nipples.
I braid sassafras leaves in my hair, bathe in hibiscus water, paint
toes with pomegranate juice.
> Mwen trape san ki soti nan lang mwen
> nan yon tas pentire po je mwen, bouch, ak pwent
> tete. Mwen trese sassafras fèy nan cheve m, benyen nan
> dlo hibiscus zòtèy penti ak ji grenad.

Lying down under cypress tree
I wait for fire ants to quiet my noisy blood.
> Kouche anba pichpen Mwen tann
> pou foumi pou boule san fè bwi mwen.

## Muscle Shoals Kinda Love
*For all my Blindian blues sistas*

You were fine and brown
tall and sleek like some
thunderbird come to make
me the next mother of mankind.
And boy did I bend.
Learning to preen and caw
cry and sing a warbling call
for this love born of memories
and music, promise and pain.

*Street corner love affairs*
*hot humid summer air*
*when we's wuz young.*
*Saturday, Sunday*
*denial of Mondays*
*havin fun—*
*Knowin you were wrong fo me—*
*but focused on your body's poetry—*

This was our sound ridin
from Florida through Alabama
to Louisiana, tires cryin,
radio wailin, spirits tailgatin
Percy croons as I think
Baby, please don't treat me bad—[xvii]

But land we travel is a beaten
trail of tears washed in blood
keepin dirt red cuz more than
one kind of rain has fallen here.
Some like tears full of salt,
some thick as blood drippin
down trees like black sap.

I was young and round runnin

from music of memories tied
to my heels by umbilical chords
that can't be severed and you were
a promise of sweet sticky heat
burning through lusty late night car rides
parked on the corner as Aretha
moans truth of you into my ears
You're a liar and you're cheat.[xviii]
This too is our song.

*Street corner love affairs*
*hot humid summer air*
*when we's wuz young.*
*Saturday, Sunday*
*denial of Mondays*
        *havin fun–*
*Knowin you were wrong fo me–*
*but focused on your body's poetry–*

This is the red/black.
Where red clay meets
black tar pavement
and the earth herself
moves to the rhythmic
shuffle step of a bump
and grind homegrown
in shell shook call and
responses peppered with
field worked gospels and
chain cried blues.

A deep worn body ache.
A get up and move groove.
A Muscle Shoals Sound
        Kinda Love.

## How to Write A NDN Country-Western Zydeco 2-Step

**I.**
(It starts wit'da squeezebox)

Set cowboy boot foot ta tapping.
Remember ya truck is a pony.
It don't run. It's always a *she*.
There ain't no cars in NDN-Zydeco country.
We can make allowances fo' *certain* crossovers.

(Guitar, Bass, and Drums).

**II.**
Your pony must have
a goot NDN name.
Follow the formula
Verb. Adjective.
*Avoid*: Bubbling,
Talking, or Rolling.
Followed by:
Wind, Breeze, Bluster.

Your busted pony is
a heart metaphor.
Example: Engine blown out
like guts on love's back road.

(enter the frottoir and spoons).

**III.**
Your man/woman, gave goot
lovin, but they done ya wrong.
Your spirit is run-over.
Follow the formula of
Literary allusion.
Simile (like) "road-kill."

Example: And I'm a
wandering blind in a
loveless desert, feelin'
flattened like armadillo
road kill.

**IV.**
(crescendo: steel lap guitar and fiddle)

Set your sites on a new catch
(man or woman).
Trick out your tired pony with
a rebuilt corroborator, tires, or battery.
Double check that your engine
is ready fo' the journey.
We don't want no stall outs.
(Take whatever means necessary
to avoid stalls, including the little
blue pills— aiiieeee).

Take down the old feathers your
ex put on the rearview. Don't
hang the plastic beaded war bonnet
(unless your lookin for a short-term
snag, white "part ndn," or are outta sweetgrass).

Make a reference ta crawdads:
*Cuz now we's suckin face*
*like crawdad head,*
*two-steppin our boots 'bout*
*headin fo' bed.*
*Broke down, worn out,*
*nuttin a little wiggle, little jiggle*
*on the dance floor, can't turn about.*

(It ends with squeezebox and guitar)

## Taste / Speak

Outside-
wraps warm
wet blanket
around my shoulders.
Dampness beads crystal
on forehead upper lip,
dampens hair
at nape, and by ears.

Breathe deep air
tastes green,
and brown, wet.
Olfactory memory
rushes, time warp.

I am young again
taste of muscadines,
wild onions, and clover
honey. My body fully
ripe as round plump
persimmons. Your hair
long waves and
dances water down
in rhythm to movement.

You are young and
taste of sugar skulls
and barely hops,
tobacco, and sweat.
My roundness bleeds
into you, meshes in a
language of rock to water.

Now I move into outer
realm of age and distance
staving stale taste of

copper and moss.
My body beginning to
drip lazily in heat.
My curves speak a
weeping willow language.

**Electric Muscadine**

Tips of fingers write electric language over
skin from peach powder soft, to firm fine brown.
Tips whorls of memory imprint swirling like
dancers round fire. Fingers leave their
mark— like stomp dancers on grass.

Examining fingers, know they are sturdy like
vines of muscadine plants— persistent, growing
in ravines, up trees, over fences, and through
years of changing climate and the push of tar
pavement through southern sun, they return.

And so, in returning, these fingers on hands,
pick muscadines. Fill baskets, buckets, holding
up hem of skirt to catch falling fruit. In these
plucking hands memory of cotton, river cane,
sugarcane, tobacco, and peanuts.

When the skin is peeled away from meat
of grape I slip it into your mouth—
Tingle of electric story slithers from fingertip
across your tongue mingling with eruption
of musk grape nectar...

# Rituals of Morning Water
*For dad*

Rising with brown arms grabbing rusty traps in water colour of hematite
gray of dawn like wet sand he makes his way to morning water.
He has gone to water every morning since he was released from water.
We rose from brackish briny estuaries, alligator people, crawdad people.

Gray of dawn like wet sand as he makes his way to morning water
without putting tongue to task, muscle memory breaths words of prayer.
We rose from brackish briny estuaries, alligator people, crawdad people
ripple a language echoed in blood, mudbug songs and gar fish two-steps.

Without putting tongue to task, muscle memory breaths words of prayer.
Sun cresting, gulf water in green-blue hue with undertone of black bruises.
Ripple a language echoed in blood, mudbug songs and gar fish two-steps,
whimpering cry under waves so soft, only heard by those of us birthed here.

Sun cresting, gulf water in green-blue hue with undertone of black bruises.
Like his wife, daughters, and mothers' wombs- earth mother is bleeding out.
Whimpering cry under waves so soft, only heard by those of us birthed here.
Ritual of morning water, crab traps and cast nets, becomes a stilted mourning.

Like his wife, daughters, and mothers' wombs- earth mother is bleeding out.
We rose through lifeblood slick birth memory so as to remember her songs.
Ritual of morning water, crab traps and cast nets, becomes a stilted mourning.
    Songs slip as fading tides from lips whose prayers sit perched like hungry
                                    pelicans.

We rose through lifeblood slick birth memory so as to remember her songs.
Gray of dawn like wet sand he makes his way to morning water,
    songs slip as fading tides from lips whose prayers sit perched like hungry
                                    pelicans.
He has gone to water every morning since he was released from water…

                To keep the language of water

## What I Know

this is what I know

dad wakes in gray
orange breaking through
salt mists on chalk
dusted Gulf

his arms are brown
his net frayed with
memories of hands
not his own but of
his blood

his knife handle
made of smoothed
cypress
blade sharpened
steel
made while courting
my mother—
of it I know nothing more

knife slides under
gills of a mullet
separating body
quickly
belly opens spilling
guts
onto pewter sand turning
black and brown
with mucus and slime

dad fills my pink
plastic beach bucket
with heads—
across the shore

sun has broken
briny air mingling with
smell of fish heads—
fiddlers scramble
while gulls pelicans
and egrets mill about
mom and I fill traps with
heads for blue crabs

later in morning mom
kisses
father dressed in oil
stained overalls and steel-toed
boots—leaving for work
as she fries mullet fillets
and eggs for sister and my
breakfast—

this is what I know

I can still smell fish
on my fingers
taste salt on my lips

## If'n I Wuz Your Pocahontas Marie Laveau
*for the NDN-Creole Wonder Septuplets*

If'n I Wuz Your Pocahontas Marie Laveau

I'da be tall risin like a goddess with willowy limbs.
My eyes would slant cat-like upwards minx a simultaneous
sexual beacon of Egyptian Africa tinted with deep green
of eastern pine trees under eagle winged black brows.

My skin would glow of amber like aged North American
sap dusky with ground black cardamom and my kiss
would be full of the heat of three guinea peppers.
My touch cool as virgin Cohongarooton tidewater.

If'n I wuz your Pocahontas Marie Laveau.

My ass would be from your finest Hottentot Venus
imagination and my hair would float a black cloak
to a waist so tiny as to be in danger of breaking
from my bountiful earth mother bosom, if not for that ass.

Oh yes I would be that dream of perfection
red-black miscegenation princess predilection.

If'n I wuz your Pocahontas Marie Laveau.

My French would show in the green of my eyes
nary the Irish cuz we know they weren't really white.
My skin would be spiced dark, but not black, my lips full,
but not flat, my hair thick, with nary a kink, and I mysterious.

But this is reality and you get me.
I'm not your NDN-Creole princess,
and my ass juts out sassy and all that then
goes flat n' dimpled like NDN frybread.
And my Irish shows, like my Choctaw, Mvskoke
My Spanish, African, Cree, and French.

But... If'n I wuz your Pocahontas Marie Laveau,
You could:

*Call me the voodoo woman...*
*the sky begin to cry—*[xix]
*And Maybe Marlon Brando will be there*
*by the fire—*[xx]
And I will throw the bones, rise with
my willowy limbs and buttocks of lust,
bounteous bosom which suckled mestizo nations.

If'n I wuz your Pocahontas Marie Laveau.

## Keeping Away Bundle

When you left
I was standing on dock
peering into hazel-hued water,
as if counting barnacled oyster shells
would distract my spirit.

At night I carve
pantoums and villanelles
up and down my legs
with an old glovers needle.

The leather of my flesh still
supple enough to slide words into.
So I make magic on skin, my body
becomes a bundle carrying tobacco, cedar,
leftover seed, bone shards, amniotic fluid.

I learn to keep moving
in shallows of salt water
so nothing can grow on my limbs.

When wading birds get too close I simply unfold myself.

Power of this
Keeping Away Bundle.

## Miscegenation Round Dance

Yu ho he˙
(yu ho he˙)
blood colour of boiled mudbugs, humid and ornery
briny as brack water fed on father's gumbo and mother's buffalo
meat
Yu ho he˙
(yu ho he˙)
wey hey ya wey yo
wey hey ya wey yo

Ain't no way you can take the bayou outta blood.
Ain't no how you can take away all the loss o'blood.
More than one story o' People survived more than one flood.

Crawdad carried mud in hands when waters rose to make land.
When waters rose, we packed bags, lost homes, returned to
crescent land.
Waves weren't always rising waters, at times tides came to separate
and ban.

When men in suits, crisp white linen sweating in Caribbean heat
Came separating us like prickly cotton from shaft in September
heat.
Kinfolk whose lines were blurred 'cross Uncle Jim found ways to
cheat—

Woven brackish blood, braided carries memory for all my
relations.
Weavings like basketry, strand for Euro, one Africa, third Indian
Nations.
Into a circle we moved to dance, taking partners, making alliances
for survival.
Delicate plans, fragile treaties' offspring, crumbled under
statehood's arrival.

Under rubble feet in fresh spring grass, rose Blindian children
survival's creations.

We danced circles of knowledge, undulating in-out double-headed
serpent.
*Chahta, Atakapa, Natchitoches*, casting nets in *bayuks*, harvesting
verdant.
In the time before the Frog People came, to dance into our circle
violently making
Woven brackish blood.

I've come to rattle the bones! Under waters where cypress roots
grow—
*Étranger blanc* who brought people in iron chains shuffling dance,
to plant and hoe,
Took us Indian women to barter, to breed and teach foreigners
the way of land.
I've come to rattle the bones! Rising up *shilup, haint,* makin'
tongues you no understand.
Wounds keloid over time wit' age, so come my Pappy, Indian wit'
nappy an' me light as sno'
Woven brackish blood.

Yu ho he˙
(yu ho he˙)
blood colour of red brick dust, sticky sweet like pralines
salty as air in afternoon Gulf showers fed on father's
beignets and mother's bannock
Keeping time to rhythm of songs drumming through
thrum of heart
Like rush of river meeting Gulf, dancing, catching honor
beats under each fall of feet

Yu ho he˙
(yu ho he˙)
wey hey ya wey yo
wey hey ya wey yo
wey hey ya wey hey ya

wey hey ya wey yo
~ he`

## Sweeping Away[xxi]

There's been a chipping off,
carving, and claiming from
waterways to inter deltas—
Second coming settlers
exploring bodies from fleshy
river banks to shaded pines.

*You've got a mouthful of gimme, a handful of much oblige*

Dwindling sands counted and stored
marked like inventory, numbered,
enrolled, verified, certified, organic—
Catalogued carefully beside red clay
and white clay samples—
Both entities whose bodies forget the
flexibility of coil pottery—
under browned silt worked hands

*You've got a mouthful of gimme, a handful of much oblige*

If the last bit of my home
sits caked down— a deep red line
under crevices of my toenails—
You would come sightseeing
only to dig it out—
Sweeping the dirt away.

*You've got a mouthful of gimme, a handful of much oblige*

## Palms Open-faced

In this space I offer you
broken threads still frayed and
raw from trauma of
sever.

I give you
palms open-faced
remnants of this
rooted place—

Salt water slipping through fingers,
river mud caked into lifeline,
a leftover muscadine skin,
and four loquat seeds.

When earth begins to shake
so loud I can no longer hear echoes of
shell shaking stomp dancers and leader calls
in southern wind ebb and flow —

And grass blades cease
vibrating delta blue rhythmic moans
against souls of my feet—

When waters, they rise
oil slick
you will find me in
Spring Bayou

Tying cursing knots in
cottonmouths.

**Rain Prud'homme:** is a writer, singer/songwriter, musician, visual artist, and winner of the First Book Award Poetry from Native Writers' Circle of the Americas, for her collection *Smoked Mullet Cornbread Crawdad Memory* (MEP 2012, published as Rain C. Goméz), An Assistant Professor of English, Affiliated Faculty, International Indigenous Studies, and Indigenous Student Access Program at University of Calgary, she is a "FATtastically Queer IndigeNerd," working primarily within Gulf Creole; Indigenous and Afro-Indigenous Studies (Louisiana Creole, First Nation/Métis/Inuit/Native American/Latinx); BIPOC Rhetorics; Fat Studies; ecocriticism; 2SQ/gender/sexuality; STEM & Literary Theory; and Creative Writing (poetry, essay, short story, and creative non-fiction). Her monograph *Gumbo Stories: Rhetorics and Quantum Relation-Making in the Creole South* is forthcoming and her co-edited collection *Louisiana Creole Peoplehood: Afro-Indigeneity and Community* will be in print 2021 from University of Washington Press and the co-edited collection *Indians, Oil, & Water: Indigenous Ecologies and Literary Resistance*, in print summer 2022 (TPHP). Rain's current creative projects include: *Epidermal Journal: Multimodal Poems*; *"I oughta know about lonely girls": Essays on Body, FAT, Love, & Place*; and critical projects: *"Nobody Loves a Fat Girl": Obesity, Obsession, Exile, and Largeness of Literary Resistance*; and *Gather at the River: Spiritual Ecologies in Red/Black Literature*. She is the Executive Editor and Publisher of That Painted Horse Press: A Borderless BIPOC Press of the Americas. Most importantly, she is an Auntie, daughter, sister, cousin, and "adopted/substitute" Auntie to a flock of graduate and former students and adopted mom to the coolest kiddo ever.

Jeffery Darensbourg PhD (Atakapa-Ishak) is a Monroe Research Fellow at the New Orleans Center for the Gulf South at Tulane University, educator, and activist. He is an enrolled member and tribal councilperson of the Atakapa-Ishak Nation of Southwest Louisiana and Southeast Texas, and is of Louisiana Creole, Ishak, and Choctaw ancestry, with family roots across South Louisiana. Darensbourg is the editor of the zine, *Bullbancha Is Still a Place: Indigenous Culture from New Orleans*, whose work has appeared in  various publications and news outlets including *Situate Magazine*, and is forthcoming in various publications. He is currently working on a monograph addressing Ishak land, culture, and language.

Cover art: "Mom hoktiwe pumblo!" by Rain Prud'homme & EL Kiki Shawnee: ""Mom hoktiwe pumblo!," Ishak for, "Let's all dance together," is a multimedia work featuring the Auntie and Niece duo of Prud'homme and Shawnee. Featuring original ledger art drawings of Creole, Ishak, Choctaw, Caddo, Quapaw, Freedmen, Creole Zydeco Musicians, Tunica Biloxi, Wichita, and Settlers, accented by original flora and fauna. Shawnee is a young emerging artist from Oklahoma working in multiple mediums including paint/ink, beadwork, basketry, clay, textiles, and photography. Shawnee has won multiple local awards for her work and is the cover artist for *Toledo Rez & Other Myths* (That Painted Horse Press 2019), by Thomas Parrie (Choctaw-Apache). Shawnee's mother is of Louisiana Creole-Ishak, Choctaw-Biloxi, Celtic, Freedmen, and métis ancestry while her father is Quapaw, Shawnee, Miami, and Cherokee. Rain Prud'homme was originally going to be an art major, but found herself drawn to language- painting with words. Prud'homme still works as a visual artist primarily in pen/ink, water colour, graphite and charcoal, mural, photography, clay, and digital paint mediums. Her art has been featured in various collections, books, and book covers.

# Notes

[i] Louisiana's Code Noir, 1723; Tattooed Serpent, Natchez Chief to Antoine Simon Le Page du Pratz recounted by Le Page du Pratz in *The Colonial Legacy, Volume 3: Historians of Nature and Man's Nature*
[ii] "Red River Valley," Edith Fowke version.
[iii] see: Barr, Juliana. *Peace Came in the Form of a Woman: Indians and Spaniards in the Texas Borderlands*. Chapel Hill: University of North Carolina, 2007.

[iv] Jeanne de la Grande Terre and Marie Anne Therese were Chitimacha slaves turn wives of Francois Guyon dit Dion Despres Derbanne and Jacques Guedon from the Natchitoches area. Marie Thérèse *ditte* Coincoin or CoinCoin was the slave concubine manumitted by Claude Thomas Pierre Métoyer. These women form matrilineal mother lines of many Cane River Louisiana Creoles.
[v] Cajun Folk Ballad, "Aux Natchitoches." English translation: "Choose the colour of ashes/ For this is the saddest colour"

[vi] Refrains from Catholic prayer to Our Lady of Prompt Succor, the patron saint of New Orleans, and excerpts from George W. Harkins' (Choctaw) letter to the American People, February 25, 1832

[vii] Records of the Attakapa District of Louisiana 1739-1811; *The Lake Charles Atakapas (cannibals) period of 1817 to 1820* by Joseph Osterman; Louisiana's Code Noir, 1723

[viii] The song, "When the Levee Breaks," by Memphis Minnie and Kansas Joe McCoy, has been in the public domain since 2004. The Song has been reworked by Led Zeppelin and Bob Dylan.

[ix] Musicians such as Richi Havens, Eric Clapton, Sweet Honey and the Rock, as well as the Louisiana mother of gospel Mahlia Jackson have reworked this traditional African American spiritual, "Motherless Child," in the modern era.
[x] Emerson Bentley, Ohio-born white school teacher, editor of *The Progress*, a Republican newspaper in Opelousas.

xi "Thomas Jefferson's Confidential Letter to Congress, January 18. 1803"; *The Indian Removal Act 1830*

xii Hammersiten II, Oscar. "Oklahoma!" Rec. 1943. *Oklahoma!: The Muscial.* MP3.

xiii In "Reply" to Joy Harjo's "Reconciliation: A Prayer"

xiv Contains refrains from "In My Time of Dying," an African American spiritual. Lines from the song first appeared in Emmet Kennedy's collection of Louisiana street performers, *Mellows- A Chronicle of Unknown Singers*, (1925), and in the Cleveland Library's *Index to Negro Spirituals*. Blind Willie Johnson recorded the song in 1927 as "Jesus Make Up My Dying Bed." Bob Dylan and Led Zepplin made the song popular in popular culture in the 60s and 70s.

xv The song, "House of the Rising Sun" is a traditional folk song, also known as "Rising Sun Blues." It is in the public domain and has been covered by The Animals, Joan Baez, and Lauren O'Connell.

xvi *The Indian Removal Act 1830*; *Plessy V Ferguson, 163 U.S. 537* (1896); House concurrent resolution 108; Public Law 959; *United States Circuit Court of Appeals EIGHTH CIRCUIT. Bettie Ligon Et Al, Appellants, vs. Douglas H. Johnston, Et Al, Appellees.* 23 May 1907.

xvii Percy Sledge's "When a Man Loves a Woman" recorded 1966 at F.A.M.E. Studio, in Muscle Shoals Alabama.

xviii Aretha Franklin's "I Never Loved a Man" recorded 1967 at F.A.M.E. Studio, in Muscle Shoals Alabama.

xix Taylor, Koko. "Voodoo Woman." Rec. 1975. *I Got What It Takes.* Koko Taylor. Bruce Iglauer, 1975. Vinyl recording.

xx Young, Neil. "Pocahontas." Rec. 1979. *Rust Never Sleeps.* Neil Young & Crazy Horse. Neil Young, David Briggs, Tim Mulligan, 1979. CD.

xxi Contains refrains from Clarence Williams, "Gulf Coast Blues' recorded by Bessie Smith in 1923.

Paternal Family Photos in order of appearance: Author's great-great grandmother; Author's great-Meemaw; Author's grandfather; Author's grandmother; Author with her father

www.ingramcontent.com/pod-product-compliance
Lightning Source LLC
Chambersburg PA
CBHW070206100426
42743CB00013B/3065